I0407243

Ethics & Professional Development for Addiction Counselors

Principles, Guidelines & Issues
for the Training, Licensing, Certification and
Re-certification of Addiction Counselors

Marcus M. Mottley, Ph.D.

Life Management Publishing

Life Management Publishing
Copyright © 2012

ISBN-13: 978-1470149352
ISBN-10: 1470149354

Limits of Liability and Disclaimer Warranty
The author and publisher shall not be liable for any misuse of this material. The information herein is for educational and informational purposes and not clinical advice. Get proper advice from licensed professionals in your jurisdiction.

Table of Contents

About the Author

Marcus M. Mottley is President of *Life Management International*, a human services and organizational consulting firm. He has over 40 years of experience in education, training, counseling, coaching and business consulting. He is a clinical psychologist and maintains a private practice in Addictions Counseling, Strategic Psychotherapy, Neuro-Linguistic Programming and Hypnotherapy.

Dr. Mottley has worked in the field of addictions treatment since 1987 and first served as an addiction counselor serving clients from the U.S. Probation office and community programs. He has conducted hundreds of workshops for addiction counselors on topics such as Ethics & Confidentiality, Professional Development, Cultural Competence, Micro-skills of Counseling, Co-Occurring Disorders, Relapse Prevention and Understanding the DSM. He has also worked in the field of drug prevention and served as the administrator for the Safe & Drug Free schools program for a large school district where he trained prevention professionals, school administrators, teachers, parents and students. He has given keynotes and conducted seminars nationally and internationally for government agencies, corporations, schools, associations and community agencies on a variety of other subjects and topics.

He is available for executive coaching, private consultations, keynote addresses, workshops, seminars, organizational development and private consultations.

What is Ethics?

There have been many different definitions of ethics. Some say that ethics is the essence of an individual. In other words according to one theorist, your essence – your essential self – is indicated by "what you do when no one is looking!"

Other theorists tie ethics to one's character as evidenced by the statement, "Ethics is honesty in action."

Other definitions focus on people's behaviors with principles such as "the end justifies the means" and "nothing is wrong if the majority decides to do it."

When most people attempt to define of ethics however, they reference words like values, morals and 'good character'.

While all of the above ideas, perspectives and definitions may serve the general public well, the definition that serves professional occupations is different. In this case, **ethics is defined as 'right conduct'** as specified by the specific profession. Thus medical doctors, lawyers, psychologists and social workers all embrace ethical guidelines as specified by the professional associations.

Ethical guidelines within a specific profession are formulated to provide moral standards for the appropriate use of skills and techniques. Ethical principles are also established to provide some assurance of safety to the public and a foundation or climate of trust in the counseling or therapeutic relationship.

In this book, the ethical guidelines and principles presented are those that govern addiction counselors specifically, and psychotherapists, social workers and psychologists, in general.

The principles, guidelines and discussions specify and frame the core expectations for the proper conduct of addiction counselors as they work in the field of addictions.

Professional vs. Unethical vs. Illegal

In some cases, professional behaviors, ethical issues and illegal behaviors all come together in one event. Take for example the case of an addiction counselor who was assigned a client by her supervisor. When the counselor read the client's social history and case file she was uncomfortable with aspects of the client's history. This client was HIV positive, a recovering alcoholic, an active cocaine and heroin user, convicted drug dealer, a convicted rapist and child sexual offender and had spent the last fourteen years incarcerated.

The counselor set an appointment with the client for an initial counseling session. However, on the day of the appointment, the counselor was stuck in rush hour traffic and arrived late for the session. When she realized that she would be late, she failed to notify her supervisor. Thus, when the supervisor realized that the client had been waiting for well over an hour rescheduled the appointment for another date. The counselor's behavior was distinctly unprofessional in being late for the appointment and failing to notify her supervisor. Her behavior would not be considered unethical.

At the next scheduled meeting, the counselor – still disturbed by the client's profile and social history – decided that she would avoid meeting the client hoping that her supervisor would reassign him to a colleague. So, on the day of the appointment she called in sick. This behavior is clearly unethical.

The supervisor in realizing that the counselor viewed the client negatively gave her an ultimatum and insisted that she reschedule the client and meet with him. The counselor's job was now on the line… so she met with the client. After several sessions, both counselor and client established a good professional rapport. However, several weeks later, the client offered the counselor money and gifts to change the results of a court ordered urinalysis report to incorrectly reflect that the client was not using drugs.

The client, who had regressed back to selling and using drugs, now had lots of money so that he could offer the counselor a significant financial bribe. The counselor accepted the money and changed the report.

The counselor's conduct was now unprofessional, unethical and illegal.

Enforcement of Ethical Principles

There are several ways in which ethical principles within the addiction counseling profession are enforced in order to protect clients from potentially harmful actions by addiction counselors.

1. Control through ***general*** criminal law. This is where both criminal proceedings can be brought against professionals by law enforcement officials for potential violations. For example, in the aforementioned case where the counselor took a bribe from a client, several criminal charges could potentially be brought against the counselor including charges for fraud and for falsifying a report to the court.

2. Control exerted on addiction counselors by their peers. Most addiction counseling professionals are members of a counseling organization or association managed by their peers. If a member of the association is found to have violated one of the ethical guidelines, the association members, through their ethics committee, could sanction the member. Sanctions could involve a timed suspension of the member's membership to a full expulsion from the association. Any sanction carries potentially serious implications for counselors since in many jurisdictions a counselor's government license or registration is based on their certification as a member of the recognized professional organization.

This is true in other helping professions such as social worker, where, depending on the area of the country, a social worker's license is largely dependent on their status as a current member of the local chapter of the National Association of Social Workers.

3. Profession-specific legal controls emerging from state licensing boards and the establishment of entry standards, definitions of practice and delineation of offenses and sanctions. State licensing boards establish the parameters under which addiction counselors practice within the specific state. If the counselor is found to have violated standards of practice as set out by the licensing board, then the counselor can be sanctioned at various levels including being de-licensed. Additionally, in some states, as indicated above, if the counselor is de-certified by their counseling board, then the state will revoke the license of the counselor.

4. Additional control through civil actions and malpractice complaints. Clients can assert their legal rights through civil suits and malpractice complaints if they believe that any of the rights have been violated.

5. Controls imposed by or derived from federal laws and regulations which may be different from state and local laws. There are federal laws which regulate the practice of counseling and which if broken, can trigger legal actions by federal institutions. The general laws governing addiction counseling in this regard are found (but not limited to) the Code of Federal Regulations (specifically 42 CFR Part 2 & 2a).

This regulation mandates that addiction treatment information in the possession of substance abuse treatment providers be handled with a greater degree of confidentiality than general medical information.

Principles of Ethics

Principle 1: Non-Discrimination

Under this principle the addiction counselor must not discriminate against clients or other professionals whether based on race, gender, age, disability, national ancestry, sexual orientation, economic condition or any other marker of identification. This is particularly important in the changing dynamics of an increasingly diversified population and where, in many cases, the cultural identity of the certified and licensed addiction professional may be totally different from the clients who need services the most.

Under this guideline, the addiction counselor must also avoid bringing personal or professional issues into the relationship.

Counselors must develop a keen sensitivity to the potentially deep and hurtful impact of stereotyping and discrimination on clients.

Additionally, irrespective of the description, background or profile of the client, the counselor must not only protect but advocate for the individual rights and personal dignity of all clients.

Accordingly, the addiction counselor must be knowledgeable about disabling conditions, **demonstrate empathy** and **personal emotional comfort** *in interactions* with clients with disabilities. This is crucially important in situations where client and counselor share radically different backgrounds and perspectives. For example, a counselor must be able to demonstrate clinical empathy with a client who has a history of rape and must demonstrate that he or she is comfortable working with clients who, in the eyes of the counselor,

8

may have been convicted of 'terrible crimes.'

Emotional comfort is the ability of the counselor to work effectively with any client irrespective of their past history. Working effectively means that the counselor will act in the best interest of the client and hold the welfare of the client as premier.

Many counselors find this challenging and some, although they give lip service to following this guideline, carry internal objections to working with clients with case history profiles that they find distasteful. In such cases, counselors are rendered less effective than they could be and are severely hampered by their perspective of the client because of their unwillingness to be empathic and their inability to demonstrate emotional comfort.

Under this guideline counselors are also guided to make available necessary accommodations that allow clients with disabilities to receive services. This is oftentimes difficult for counselors since client accommodations are the responsibility of the organization rather than the individual client. Yes… it is the organization's obligation to fully comply with the American with Disabilities Act. However, it is the counselor's obligation to properly represent the interests of the client and as such, if the rights of the clients are being violated by the organization, counselors should be able to demonstrate that they have represented the needs and concerns of clients to their organizations. The best way for counselors to do this is in writing to their supervisors and company officials and documenting such actions in their client records.

However it is done, counselors should maintain documentary evidence that they have advocated on behalf of their clients.

Principle 2: Responsibility

The Principle of Responsibility contends that the addiction counselor must demonstrate objectivity and integrity, and practice the highest standards in all services that are offered.

Addiction counselors are asked to respect their organization's rules and policies as they carry out their duties as employees. However, counselors are expected to advocate for improvement of practices and policies to serve the best interests of clients.

Counselors are also seen as educators and as such they have a primary obligation to educate clients, other customers and colleagues with respect to the field of addiction counseling.

Addiction counselors who supervise other counselors have an obligation to help their supervisees to increase their knowledge and skills. In this regard, supervisees should facilitate the professional development of their staff and provide accurate and current information on addiction topics.

The supervising addiction counselor also has an obligation to provide timely performance evaluations and be supportive in giving supervisees effective supervision and consultation regarding their caseload.

This principle places high levels of obligation on counselors. Primarily, counselors are considered the first level of protection for clients and as such all counselor activities ought to be conducted in the best interests of clients.

Counselors also have an obligation to their peers in their association and in the field to be watchful that the highest standards of conduct are maintained and upheld by colleagues. Here too, counselors are the first level of protection and representation – this time for their colleagues in the field of addiction counseling.

Therefore, in keeping with the above, addiction counselors who become aware of unethical conduct, unprofessional behavior, questionable modes of conduct, or illegal activities of their peers are obligated to report such behaviors or activities to the appropriate authorities, including but not limited to the ethics committees of their counseling association.

Principle 3:   Competence

Addiction counseling, social work and psychotherapy are all founded on national standards of competency. For example, the qualifications and training requirements for a Level 1 Counselor is generally the same from one state to another. This makes it easy for states to reciprocate in the process of licensing, registering or certifying counselors from another state.

Because the field is founded on national standards of competency, addiction counselors must recognize and accept the need for a specific level of knowledge, training, expertise and experience at their specific levels of qualification. This entails not only entry level knowledge at the time of certification, but ongoing training, skill development and fine tuning of their levels of competency.

While addiction counselors strive to improve their knowledge, skills and overall competency they must also recognize their current levels of limitation. In so doing they are cautioned to match the services they offer to clients with their level of knowledge and skills and not attempt to use techniques that are outside of their current professional areas of competence. For example, an addiction counselor should not engage in Dialectical Behavioral Therapy without the requisite training and certification.

The issue of competence is not only related to levels of knowledge and skill but to the level of functioning of the addiction professional. As such counselors must acknowledge that their own personal problems may impair them and interfere with their professional effectiveness. In such cases, counselors are asked to seek the appropriate treatment for their problem.

This principle also supports the imperative identified by most counseling associations that their members aggressively pursue continuing education in the field. One of the problems that plague addiction counseling in particular is the fact that many of the counselors in some states fulfill the minimum education requirement for certification. As a result, there are potentially thousands of counselors in various parts of the country who are not familiar with the new and emerging advancements in the treatment of addictions.

This issue is of critical importance because of the fact that these minimally informed counselors are providing services based on 'ancient', out of date, and often ineffective modes of counseling. This has a direct negative impact on client outcomes.

Principle 4: Legal & Moral Standards

Addiction counselors are expected to uphold all legal and moral codes which pertain to the performance of their duties in the profession. In order to do this, counselors must be fully familiar with all local, state and federal laws which apply to the profession.

Counselors are asked not claim either directly or by implication, professional qualifications or affiliations that they do not possess. Counselors are solely responsible for this and cannot pass on this obligation to their employers or other parties. For example, an organization hires a Master's level counselor and provides him with a business card that identifies him with a doctoral degree. It is the counselor's responsibility to return the card and have it changed to the appropriate degree.

This responsibility is also attached to all products and services that the counselor offers including workshops, counseling sessions, publications and other media including online information. All references related to the counselor must meet all of the ethical standards discussed in the code of ethics for addiction counselors.

Ethics and the Law

There are several differences between legal violations and ethical violations. Ethical problems may occur either willfully or inadvertently. Such problems may result when guidelines are ambiguous and there is general confusion about how to deal with certain situations. An important distinction between ethics and the law is that the law must consider the degree of negligence or intent of the act. However, in ethical violations, particularly in the counseling professions, qualifying factors are rarely considered when judging the behavior of professionals. Just as ignorance of the law is not an acceptable defense, unfamiliarity with applicable ethical principles of addiction counseling is inexcusable.

With regards to individual counselors who may be involved with law enforcement and the courts, conviction of a **misdemeanor** does not necessarily result in an ethical charge by the counseling association against an addiction counselor. Conviction of a **felony** however, maybe sufficient grounds for both de-certification, de-licensure, and expulsion from state and national associations, regardless of relevance of the crime to the counselor's professional identity.

Primarily, as indicated above, the first actions against the counselor's status as a professional will most likely be brought by his/her counseling association. The rationale behind this is twofold: When a person who happens to be an addiction counselor commits an act that has serious consequences, it is reasoned that his/her professional fitness and competence should be questioned as well.

On the other hand, if a person's behavior is particularly

egregious or is highly publicized with reference to the person's identity as an addiction counselor, then public trust in the profession and in counselors as professionals may be compromised. Counseling associations demand that their members should be role models of their profession. Therefore, very negative events or activities perpetrated by members would potentially bring all counselors into disrepute.

Principle 5: Public Statements

When making public statements – whether in speaking or in writing, addiction counselors are asked to respect the limitations of current levels of knowledge with respect to addiction counseling. Counselors are required to clearly identify information in their counseling or educational sessions as either their personal opinions or empirically validated facts and have the data to support their statements.

Public statements can include brochures, books, resumes, grant applications, advertising and promotions, blogs, and websites.

Counselors are warned against making false or fraudulent claims regarding their qualifications, training, competence, degrees and other credentials, affiliations or the services they provide.

Principle 6: Publication Credit

When addiction counselors publish any type of written, audio or visual works, they are required to assign credit to those who have contributed to the published materials.

Addiction counselors must also recognize joint authorship and major contributions. Acknowledgement should also be placed in footnotes, introductory statements or bibliographic references. Counselors should also follow copyright laws and should recognize minor contributions along with clerical and other contributions.

Principle 7: Client Welfare

The best interest and welfare of clients should be held as paramount and the ultimate concern of all addiction counselors. Therefore, counselors must promote the protection of the health, safety and welfare of all clients. All decisions or recommendations concerning client information, client progress, referral, treatment and aftercare related to the client flows from this preeminent position.

Counselors are required to disclose their professional loyalties, responsibilities and affiliations, and the code of ethics that pertain to them.

Addiction counselors are also expected to terminate the counseling relationship when it is reasonably clear that the client is not benefitting from the relationship. This obligation is one that is particularly difficult for many counselors since, most often, they are not the ones who ultimately decide on the term or termination of the counseling relationships. In consideration of this, the alternative is that client's should discuss the client's progress with their supervisor and should keep a record of their recommendations and overall discussions.

Counselors are warned not to use or encourage a client's participation in any demonstration, research or other non-treatment activities when such participation would have potentially harmful consequences for the client or when the client is not fully informed.

Counselors are also advised to provide services in environments that ensure the privacy and safety of the client at all times and they should ensure the appropriateness and quality of the services provided. This is another issue where counselors who are employed by an agency must depend on their employer to ensure private and safe counseling environments. However, under this principle, this fact does not relieve counselors of their obligation, and therefore, they must advocate for appropriate settings in which counseling takes place.

This is potentially a larger issue than it seems, since in many offices around the country, addiction counseling takes place in settings where there is minimal privacy: e.g. cubicles with flimsy, low partitions.

Principle 8: Confidentiality

Confidentiality is one of the most important aspects of the counselor-client relationship. Confidentiality in this case is an ethical principle rather than a legal one. As an ethical principle, the counselor is expected to protect client information from disclosure without the consent of the client. In the context of counseling, confidentiality is important because it helps to provide a 'psychologically safe environment', climate or setting such that the client can 'explore difficult aspects of their lives and their selves. Without this 'psychologically safe' climate, clients might be reluctant to share private and deeply personal information about themselves and their significant others. As a result, without free and unrestricted sharing counseling would be seriously limited as a beneficial therapeutic experience.

Additionally, as will be discussed later in this text, confidentiality is also a legal right under several Federal regulations. In this regard, a legal right exists for clients which prohibits their information from being disclosed without their properly executed consent.

Counselors must provide clients their rights regarding confidentiality, in writing. Counselors must also inform clients about any areas that may be likely to affect confidentiality. In other words, the counselor must inform the client of circumstances that are likely to reduce or undermine the expectation of confidentiality. This includes the recording of the clinical interview, the use of material for insurance purposes, and the use of material for training or observation by another party. See Exceptions to Confidentiality below.

21

Counselors are expected to make appropriate provisions for the maintenance of confidentiality and the ultimate disposition of confidential records. This is another circumstance where counselors are obligated to ensure that their agencies are fulfilling this requirement on their behalf.

The security of client information is critical and only data that is necessary and appropriate for the services being provided should be accessed. Information that is stored in filing cabinets should be secured with locks, while information that is stored electronically should be robustly protected by redundant security systems.

Counselors should discuss client information only in the appropriate settings for professional purposes that are in the client's best interest. Every effort should be made to avoid undue invasion of the client's privacy. Client information includes data and reports accessed from other organizations as well as information generated through the counselor or his agencies activities including counseling session notes, mental health assessments, medical reports and reports on urinalysis results.

There are many situations where external organizations seek information about the client and are given the appropriately executed consent by the client. However, such written and oral reports must present only data germane and pursuant to the purpose of the evaluation, diagnosis, purpose or compliance of the report. Again, every effort must be made to avoid undue invasion of the client's privacy. Information that is not pertinent to the nature and type of request – or related to the purpose of the request – should be excluded from any report.

Addiction counselors are also cautioned in the use of clinical, counseling and other materials in teaching and or writing and ensure that the information used cannot identify clients.

Confidentiality vs. Privilege

As indicated above confidentiality as discussed in this book, primarily refers to a standard of professional conduct in which addiction counselors are constrained from revealing information gained within the therapeutic setting.

Privilege, or privileged communication, is a legal right that prevents information obtained in the therapeutic setting from forced disclosure to a court or others. In most situations, the client is the holder of the privilege; that is the client must sign a waiver for release of information gained with the context of the therapy.

While privilege is a legal right, confidentiality is an ethical issue. The following case exemplifies the boundaries between privilege and confidentiality.

The Jaffee Case

In Jaffee v. Redmond, the U.S. Supreme Court ruled on June 13, 1996 that communications between licensed psychotherapists and their clients are privileged and therefore protected from forced disclosure in cases arising under federal law. This was a victory for mental health organizations because it extended the confidentiality privilege on a Federal level to psychotherapists.

In this case, an on-duty police officer Mary Lu Redmond, shot and killed a knife-wielding suspect, Ricky Allen, while attempting an arrest in order to prevent him from harming another person with whom he had an argument.

Allen's family sued in Federal Court, alleging that his constitutional rights had been violated.

During discovery for the trial, Jaffee, the family's legal representative found out that Redmond had been having counseling sessions with a licensed clinical social worker. The court ordered the licensed clinical social worker to turn over notes she made during counseling sessions with Redmond after the shooting.

Ms. Redmond objected to the disclosure asserting that the contents of her conversations with the clinical social worker were protected against involuntary disclosure by psychotherapist – client privilege which she contended existed.

The court rejected her claim of psychotherapist-client privilege and the jury awarded the family $545,000.

The Court of Appeals for the Seventh Circuit then reversed this decision and concluded that the trial court had erred by refusing to afford protection to the confidential communications between Redmond and the licensed clinical social worker.

Jaffee, the legal representative of the victim's estate, appealed this decision to the Supreme Court.

The Supreme Court upheld the appellate court's decision, clarifying for all federal court cases, both civil and criminal, the existence of the privilege. The Court recognized a broadly defined psychotherapist –client privilege and further clarified that this privilege is not subject to the decision of a judge on a case by case basis. The Court's decision to extend federal privilege left the door open to other licensed counselors.

In the majority opinion of the Court, it was argued that "Effective psychotherapy depends upon an atmosphere of confidence and trust in which the patient is willing to make a frank and complete disclosure of facts, emotions, memories, and fears. Because of the sensitive nature of the problems for which individuals consult psychotherapists, disclosure of confidential communication made during counseling sessions may cause embarrassment or disgrace. For this reason, the mere possibility of disclosure may impede disclosure of the confidential relationship necessary for successful treatment."

Alternatively, "if there existed no privilege for communications between psychotherapists and their patients, people would decide not to seek treatment for mental illness, particularly illnesses and traumas that are likely to result in litigation."

Confidentiality in Multi-Client Situations

Group psychotherapy: Group members are not professionals and are not, therefore, bound by legal or ethical requirements. In all multi-client situations, it is important that the therapist establish his/her policy regarding confidentiality early in the treatment process. However, while counselors and their organizations can establish rules and policies for clients asking them to hold their discussions private, such rules did not have any value under these ethical guidelines.

In other words, while clients may stand the risk of expulsion from treatment or some other penalty for inappropriately sharing information discussed in their group settings, that issue is not a matter that has any bearing on ethics for addiction counselors. What is important is that counselors do not infringe on the rights to confidentiality of their clients.

Third-Party Access to Client Information

In cases where other agencies, insurance companies, family members, court officials, lawyers or litigants seek privileged information about a client, the counseling professional should not surrender any material until legal counsel is sought. Counselors should always consider getting their own legal representative instead of depending on their agency's lawyers. The primary, secondary and tertiary obligations of those lawyers are to the agency and its interests.

In these matters, the rights of the clients are always the primary consideration and any submission of client information or documentations should be preceded by an appropriately executed consent form signed by the client.

Addiction counselors must be cautious about the type of information released to insurance companies, for example, even if the client has consented. Many clients are not aware of the implications and dangers that releasing their information to outside parties poses. It is the counselor's obligation to educate the client about these dangers. External companies have little or no obligations to hold maintain the privacy of client data. Once this data is released, it can often be considered to be in the public domain where an insurance and or other company may share the client information with other companies.

In the event that the client is a minor, and where schools request information, the addiction counselor should release only information that will help the school better serve the child/client. In such cases, the child's legal guardians must sign the consent form.

Minors

When a client is a child, (or a person deemed to be legally incompetent or decisionally incapable) parents or guardians may be entitled to legal access to information about the client.

Even if parents hold the privilege when a minor is in counseling, counselors must exercise their own judgment with regard to "taking special care to protect the client's best interest." If for example a child does not want a parent to know about an incident or a health condition, counselors would need to exercise caution. If the parent requests information, counselors are generally expected to comply since the parent is the holder of the privilege. However, when, how and under what circumstances they release the information should reflect skillful and creative timing and strategy.

In cases involving pregnancy or drug/alcohol use, depending on the legal jurisdiction, the counselor, with extreme caution, may exercise judgment in disseminating information to the holder of the privilege with or without the consent of the client. In some states, this discretion is not left up to counselors since these states have laws which obligate counselors to release such information (particularly if it is requested). Withholding certain types of information from parents and guardians should be a decision where the agency's privacy officer, clinical supervisor and in some cases, the agency's lawyers are all involved.

In cases of child abuse, however, all states require that the counselor make a report to the proper agency. This does not imply that the counselor must inform the parents particularly if one or both of them may be implicated in the abuse.

From the beginning of the counseling relationship, the addiction counselor should discuss the nature of the confidential relationship with all parties including minor clients so that all are aware of the exceptions to confidentiality. It should be made clear, in writing, what type of information can be shared and with whom.

Duty to Warn & the Tarasoff Decision

This case was brought to court by the parents of Tatiana Tarasoff, a student at the University of California's Berkley Campus.

According to the record, Tatiana Tarasoff and Prosenjit Podar were students at the University and had met at an on-campus folk dancing class where they saw each other regularly at class. On one occasion Ms. Tarasoff kissed Mr. Podar who took this to mean that they were in a committed relationship. Ms. Tarasoff indicated to him that she was seeing other men and that she was not interested in an intimate relationship with him.

Mr. Podar felt rejected and reportedly began to stalk her with the goal of avenging her rejection. He apparently became depressed and had an emotional breakdown, speaking disjointedly and having crying spells. He began to neglect his studies, health and well-being and his studies.

During the summer of 1969 Ms. Tarasoff left the country and visited South America. During this time Mr. Podar, began to show signs of improving and on the advice of a friend, began to see a psychologist at the University of California at Berkley's Cowell Memorial Hospital. During one of their sessions he revealed to the psychologist of his intention to kill Ms. Tarasoff.

The psychologist informed the police by phone and by letter, and told of the threat and of his assessment that his client was dangerous and that he be 'civilly committed as a dangerous person'. He assessed that Podar was suffering from severe and acute paranoid schizophrenia. The police detained Mr. Podar, but he was found to be rational at the time of questioning and was subsequently released on promising to stay away from Ms. Tarasoff.

Ms. Tarasoff returned from South America but was never made aware of the threat to her life.

The psychologist did not hear from Mr. Podar again.

However, Mr. Podar befriended Ms. Tarasoff's brother even moving in with him. When he had the chance he stabbed Ms. Tarasoff to death.

Under the Tarasoff decision the therapist must first accurately diagnose the client's tendency to behave in dangerous ways towards others. This first duty is judged by the standards of professional negligence. In this case, the therapist did not fail in this duty. He even took the additional step of requesting that the dangerous person be detained and committed by the campus police. But the court held that simply notifying the police was insufficient to protect the identifiable victim.

The California Supreme court held that the psychologist had a duty not only to warn the police, but had a duty to protect Ms. Tarasoff with regard to her impending danger.

This decision is a landmark decision within the United States and is widely accepted in most jurisdictions.

The Bradley Case

In this case, the patient Mr. Wessner had been voluntarily admitted to a facility for psychiatric care. He was very upset by his wife's extramarital affair and had repeatedly threatened to kill her and her lover, and had even admitted to a therapist that he was carrying a weapon in his car for that purpose.

He was given an unrestricted weekend pass to visit his children who were living with his wife. He met his wife and her lover in the home and shot and killed them both.

His children filed a wrongful death suit alleging that the psychiatric center had breached a duty to exercise control over Mr. Wessner.

The Georgia Supreme Court (*Bradley Center v. Wessner*, 1982) ruled that a physician has a duty to take reasonable care to prevent a potentially dangerous patient from inflicting harm. According to the court's ruling, "where the course of treatment of a mental patient involves an exercise of 'control' over him by a physician who knows or should know that the patient is likely to cause bodily harm to others, an independent duty arises from that relationship and falls upon the physician to exercise that control with such reasonable care as to prevent harm to others at the hands of the patient."

Informed Consent

Informed consent is the process of ensuring that the client's values and preferences govern the care provided. Informed consent is the foundation of all counseling since it gives the client the autonomy to make the decisions about their own care and the services that they will receive. It fundamentally places the client as the sole person responsible for their care.

Counselors are obligated to explicitly explain all aspects of the client's treatment and the services that are being offered. The counselor in considering the welfare of the client, should go beyond and explain not only what the client's choices are but the potential consequences of possible decisions. Counselors must accept the fact that the clients are in charge of their treatment and that counselors serve in the role of expert advisors – not decision makers!

The core idea behind informed consent is that adult persons who are "of sound mind" have the right to consent to or refuse care, even if the result of that refusal is death.

Decisional capacity or *de facto competence* is when the individual has the ability to weigh the risks, benefits and alternatives of treatment. It requires an individual assessment of knowledge and the ability to demonstrate an adequacy of good judgment.

Legal competence signifies a generic judgment by society of when a person legally becomes an adult and is regarded as able to make binding, independent decisions.

Adult clients who are decisionally capable must be informed on a variety of critical issues before they become involved in counseling. For minors or clients who have been deemed legally incompetent or decisionally incapable, their guardians (or whoever holds the legal privilege) must be informed on behalf of the client.

The following checklist can be used as a guide in deciding on the information which must be shared with clients. It is recommended that all of the following be given to the client in writing.

Checklist for Informed Consent

1. *Voluntary participation:* The client muse be acting freely in making the decision to be involved in the counseling program. In cases where clients are mandated by courts to attend counseling, it is considered that the clients have not been coerced but have agreed with the court to do so. Clients have the prerogative to leave reject the agreement and face the consequences of their decision.

2. *Client involvement:* Clients should be informed about the level, time, effort and quality of involvement that is expected of them.

3. *Counselor involvement:* Clients should be informed about what counselors will provide and how those services will be provided. Clients should also be advised on the agency's policies on issues such as emergencies.

4. *No guarantees can be offered.* Counselors cannot offer any guarantees about client outcomes.

5. *Risks associated with counseling:* Counselors should inform clients about some of the risks associated with counseling. These may include 'exceptions to confidential information'

such as confidentiality in group and family settings. Other risks may include the fact that during counseling, clients may get in touch with repressed memories or have serious cathartic experiences.

6. *Confidentiality and privilege:* Counselors should provide a summarized explanation of the differences between confidentiality and privilege, and inform the client of his/her rights specific to each.

7. *Exceptions of confidentiality:* Counselors are to give clients a comprehensive list of the exceptions to confidentiality (partial list below).

8. *Counseling approach or theories:* Counselors must advise the client of the general counseling approaches, theories and techniques that are offered by the agency.

9. *Counseling records:* Clients must be informed about the management and eventual disposition of client records. Issues such as security and staff access should be discussed. Counselors should also inform clients on the length of time that agencies are legally required to keep client records and advise them on the methods of ultimate disposal of such records.

10. *Ethical guideline:* Clients are to be informed of the specific code of ethics which guide the conduct of their counselors.

11. *Licensing regulations:* Counselors should also notify clients of the specific jurisdictional (state or county) regulations under which they are licensed.

12. *Credentials*: Counselors should inform clients of their credentials and levels of education, training, and experience in the field of addiction counseling.

13. Fees and charges: Clients should be advised on the agencies policies regarding fees and other charges which they are expected to pay. Clients should also be advised on how financial records are kept, and who has access to such records.

14. Insurance reimbursement: If insurance companies are involved, clients should be advised as to the nature of the relationship with such companies. Clients should also be informed regarding issues such as copayments and responsibility for filing claims. In such cases, clients should also be informed as to who has the ultimate responsibility for payment (if for example the insurance company refuses to pay for services rendered to the client).

15. Disputes and complaints: Clients should be advised on how disputes (with counselors or other agency staff) should be handled.

16. *Cancellation* Policy: Agency cancellation policies should be made clear. This would involve rules regarding how much notice either party should give if sessions have to be rescheduled. Other issues would involve policies regarding weather, personal emergencies, etc. If the counselor is in private practice or if the agency charges clients directly, the client should be advised as to whether or not fees are incurred for cancellations.

17. Affiliation relationship: Clients must be clearly advised on the affiliations and relationships that counselors and/or their agencies have developed with contractors, HMO's, government agencies and research institution. Third party access to client record is a specific area of concern which must be outlined in writing.

18. Supervisory relationship: The names and official contact information of supervisors and agency officials should be made available to clients. Clients should also be informed that supervisors have unrestricted access to client records including counseling notes and reports.

19. *Colleague consultation:* Clients must also be informed that form time to time other counselors might have access to client information and that as a general standard of practice, colleague consultations occurs for training purposes and to ensure quality of care in counseling.

Exceptions to Confidentiality and Privilege

Confidentiality is not always absolute and there are several conditions where exceptions to confidentiality apply and information can or must be released to third parties – without the consent of the client.

1. Danger to self or others (duty to warn and protect): Information will be released if the counselor believes that the client is a danger to himself or others and it is necessary to release information that will protect the client or others. However, even in this case, the counselor will release only

the information that is needed to deal with the matter;

2. The client makes a written request for release of information specifying exactly what information is to be released and the length of time the release will be in effect;

3. Court ordered disclosures of records or subpoenas that are either unchallenged or overruled;

4. Systematic clinical supervision or peer consultation is an integral facet of counseling where client information is discussed among the clinical staff of an agency.

5. Clerical assistance (e.g. managed care) occurs when clerical staff have access to confidential client information so that files can be managed and secured, or where information has to be processed and or recorded. Because of current Federal regulations (HIPAA Laws) this practice does not pose a serious threat to the confidentiality of client data;

6. If legal or clinical consultation or advice is sought by the client, counselor or the counseling agency, specific information related to such activity might have to be released'

7. If the client raises issues in a law suit involving the counselor or the agency, crucial information might be released to address the issue;

8. When third parties are in the room: group sessions or family sessions;

9. If the client is a minor – the legal guardian holds the privilege and would have legal access to client information;

10. In medical emergencies the counselor or the agency may release information that is necessary to protect and ensure client health and safety.

11. When the counselor suspects *abuse* or *neglect* of a child, an elderly person, resident of an institution, a disabled adult or a decisionally incapable person, information must be released in the reporting of the abuse or neglect.

12. Counselors or agencies might potentially have to release information to a third party in order to collect a debt which is owed to them for services rendered to the client.

If clients decide to revoke consent they can do so in writing at any time.

42 CFR

The Code of Federal Regulations (CFR) is the codification of the general and permanent rules published in the Federal Register by the executive departments and agencies of the Federal Government. The Federal law and regulations severely restrict communications about identifiable clients by "programs" providing substance use/abuse diagnosis, treatment, or referral for treatment (42 CFR Part 2)

The purpose of the law and regulations is to decrease the risk that information about individuals in recovery will be disseminated and that they will be ostracized or subjected to discrimination. These regulations cover any program or agency that provides alcohol or drug abuse diagnosis, treatment, or referral for treatment and which is federally assisted, directly or indirectly.

This includes agencies that:

- Operate under a contract with any department or agency of the United States;

- Operate under a license, certificate, registration or authorization granted by any department or agency of the United States;

- Are supported by funds provided by any department or agency of the United States;

- Are assisted by the IRS of the Department of the Treasury through the allowance of income tax deductions and tax exempt status;

Confidentially often becomes confusing and complex. The following are important points regarding client confidentiality:

1. Signing of Releases: Before any information can be disclosed about a client, clients are required to sign releases, which indicate the following:
   a. What specific information will be shared?
   b. The specifics regarding with whom this information will be shared.
   c. The release must indicate that information being shared may not be   re-released to another party without the informed written consent of the client.
   d. The releases must contain time frames and dates of expiration.
   e. Clients need to know that they can revoke the release at any time.

2. Confidentiality regulations restrict the acknowledgement or denial that client has been admitted for treatment.

3. Client's rights to confidentiality need to be clearly explained to the Client

4. To safeguard confidentiality the following precautions need to be taken with support staff.
   a. Clerical staff at the treatment centers need to be clearly instructed about confidentiality of records and written correspondence, and clients admissions to or participation in treatment programs.
   b. Support staff must be instructed about confidentiality.
   c. Staff must respect confidentiality and not ask clients about who attended meetings.

5. Visitors to treatment centers and groups need to be instructed about the confidentially guidelines.

6. The clients in treatment centers and groups need to be instructed regarding confidentiality as it relates to other patients.

7. Counselors must be careful to always demonstrate professional behavior and not carelessly talk about clients in public places or discuss clients within the earshot of other clients.

No alcohol and drug abuse patient records whether identified by the nature and purpose of the records or the function of the record-keeper, are covered by these regulations *unless* the diagnosis, treatment, or referral for treatment with which the records are connected is *federally assisted.*

HIPAA

HIPAA (Health Information Portability and Accountability Act) is a federal law that protects health information. Federal standards are in place that ensure clients have access to their own medical records while adding new responsibilities to those charged with protecting this information. Under HIPAA, clients must not only have access their own records, but they have the right to know who has accessed their records over the preceding six years.

If either of these rights are not adequately provided for, clients have the right to lodge complaints and force those in possession of this data to make it available to them. Conversely, if clients find out their information was accessed by parties who should not have access to it, clients now have the right to demand both civil and criminal penalties under the HIPAA's Privacy Rule.

The Health Insurance Portability and Accountability Act of 1996 (HIPAA) required the Secretary of the U.S. Department of Health and Human Services (HHS) to develop regulations protecting the privacy and security of certain health information. To fulfill this requirement, HHS published what are commonly known as the HIPAA Privacy Rule and the HIPAA Security Rule.

The Privacy Rule, or *Standards for Privacy of Individually Identifiable Health Information*, establishes national standards for the protection of certain health information. The Privacy Rule standards address the use and disclosure of individuals' health information—called "protected health information" by organizations subject to the Privacy Rule — called "covered entities," as well as standards for

41

individuals' privacy rights to understand and control how their health information is used.

The *Security Standards for the Protection of Electronic Protected Health Information* (the Security Rule) establish a national set of security standards for protecting certain health information that is held or transferred in electronic form. The Security Rule operationalizes the protections contained in the Privacy Rule by addressing the technical and non-technical safeguards that organizations ("covered entities") must put in place to secure individuals' "electronic protected health information" (e-PHI).

"Covered Entities" include clinics, treatment centers, doctors, dentists, therapists, counselors, psychologists, insurance companies, HMO's, government programs that pay for Medicaid and Medicare, veterans' health care programs, nursing homes and pharmacies.

Information that is protected includes:

- Information that doctors, psychologists, counselors, nurses, and other health care providers put in client's health records;

- Conversations that doctors, counselors and psychologists and others have about client/patient care, or treatment with nurses and other health care professionals;

- Information about clients in the health insurer's computer system;

- Most other health information about clients held by those who must follow these laws.

Ways in which your information is protected:

- Covered entities must put in place safeguards to protect clients' health information.

- Covered entities must reasonably limit uses and disclosures to the minimum necessary to accomplish their intended purpose.

- Covered entities must have contracts in place with their contractors and others ensuring that they use and disclose clients' health information properly and safeguard it appropriately.

- Covered entities must have procedures in place to limit who can view and access clients' health information as well as implement training programs for employees about how to protect clients' health information.

Clients' Rights Under the Privacy Rule

Clients have a right to:

- Ask to see and get a copy of their health records;

- Have corrections added to their health information;

- Receive a notice that tells them how their health information may be used and shared;

- Decide if they want to give permission before their health information can be used or shared for certain purposes, such as for marketing;

- Get a report on when and why their health information was shared for certain purposes;

- File a complaint with their provider or health insurer or file a complaint with the U.S. Government if they believe that their rights have been violated.

Principle 9: Client Relationships

Counselors are responsible for maintaining and safeguarding a quality professional relationship with clients which is characterized by the highest level of integrity and ethical values.

Counselors should also make sure that clients are receiving the best quality of counseling services and ensure that clients are getting accurate and complete information about the nature of the relationship.

Sexual Intimacies with Clients

Addiction counselors are constrained from engaging in sexual activities with current clients and should not accept as clients anyone with whom they have engaged in sexual behaviors. Sexual intimacies with clients clearly represents taking advantage of a position of power. There are no ethically valid exceptions to this principle.

There are however, several mixed positions taken on this matter across the broad scope of counseling. Some associations allow counselors to be involved with former clients two (2) years after the professional relationship has ended while other associations mandate five (5) years.

A review of the literature on sexual intimacy in counseling revealed that male counselors were involved in sexual intimacies significantly more than were female counselors (approximately 9% versus 2%). A national study found that 87% of counselors and psychotherapists had been attracted to at least one client during their tenure as professionals and that 9.4% of men and 2.5% of women had acted on their feelings. Several research studies clearly show that the overall effects of sexual intimacy are negative, ranging from clients experiencing difficulty in trusting a subsequent therapist to clients committing suicide.

In addition to prohibiting sexual relationships with current clients, counselors are also warned against having sexual relationships with the romantic partners or family members of clients.

Harassment

Harassment may be defined as the act of systematic and/or continued unwanted and annoying actions of one party or a group, including threats and demands. Harassment can be verbal, physical and *psychological*.

Sexual Harassment

In the context of counseling services, sexual harassment is defined as the counselor's behavior of a sexual nature that is interpreted/perceived to be bothersome, demeaning, irritating, disrespectful or offensive. The behavior can occur in conjunction with the counselor's activities or role as a professional in a counseling agency (e.g. administrator, colleague, co-worker, consultant, educator, counselor, researcher, supervisor, etc.) in the various settings in which the addiction counseling services are provided (e.g. agency, hospital, private practice, organization, etc.).

Behaviors construed to be inappropriate and forms of sexual harassment may reflect a loss of objectivity of the addiction counselor and could result in harmful long-lasting emotional and psychological effects for the client. *Counselors should be aware that sexual harassment can be interpreted/perceived by a client regardless of the counselor's intent.*

Addiction counselors should also be aware of and be sensitive to the cultural contexts of the individual client, e.g., ethnicity, gender, religion, sexual orientation, social class, etc., when addressing sexual issues and be aware that this area can be sensitive and require attention to the client's feelings, ideas and cultural perspectives.

The foregoing needs to be clearly stated: Addiction counselors are to refrain from making sexual advances and *insinuations* that are inappropriate and offensive, *or that could be perceived* as such.

Managers and supervisors are **obligated** to conduct *prompt* and *thorough investigations* of <u>any</u> allegations of harassment, and to *procedurally* refer the matter to the appropriate office for further investigation and action.

Sexual harassment is a very serious charge that could result in the counselor being decertified, de-licensed, losing his/her job and being charged with professional misconduct.

Examples of sexual harassment may include but are not limited to:

- Sexual jokes, teasing, making inappropriate comments about an individual's body, or showing explicit pictures.

- Unwanted or unnecessary touching or making expressions, which may reasonably be interpreted as being seductive or sexually demeaning.

- Asking a person for sexual favors for example as part of a "quid pro quo" arrangement.

- Sitting too close, initiating hugging or holding of the individual.

- Dressing in a style inconsistent with what would be considered appropriate in a professional setting, e.g., a provocative style that lacks professionalism and/or is insensitive to the individual's background or culture.

Here are some recommendations on how to avoid complaints of sexual harassment:

- Become familiar with and follow the policy and guidelines for the avoidance of sexual harassment at your places of employment.

- Take a continuing education course or attend a workshop for the prevention of sexual harassment to become familiar with the issues.

- For those in private practice, develop and post your policy and guidelines for the prevention of sexual harassment.

- Demonstrate respect for your clients, their family, your colleagues and your staff.

- Think before acting; asking yourself if your words or actions could be misinterpreted. Develop the habit of reflecting on your comments and behaviors. Use a questioning mindset and ask: "Could my comments and actions be misinterpreted?"

- When feasible, addiction counselors should attempt to design the physical space in a manner that is sensitive to issues of privacy and confidentiality yet balanced by these concerns.

- Dress professionally and appropriately. Develop a written policy that requires clients to dress appropriately also.

Dual Relationships

Dual relationships occur when an addiction counselor has more than one type of relationship with a client, such as:

- A professional relationship and a prior personal relationship

- A business relationship that develops during a professional relationship

- Social or personal relationships that develop during a professional relationship

- Differing professional relationships, such as performing custody evaluations with patients or clients who are in other treatment or business relationships

- A combination of a professional and sexual relationship with a client represents a "dual relationship" which violates professional and ethical obligations.

Addiction counselors must acknowledge the power of their position with respect to their clients. They must also be aware that

49

this powerful position obligates them to avoid exploiting the trust of the client.

Addiction counselors must make every effort to avoid dual or multiple relationships with clients. Some jurisdictions allow some flexible in the foregoing and state that counselors should avoid such relationships where their 'professional judgment may be impaired' and where there is a 'risk of harm to the client'.

Some associations warn that if an addiction counselor is contemplating the establishment of a dual relationship with a current or former client that he/she takes the additional step of seeking consultation with their association, a supervisor or from an esteemed colleague.

Counselors are further advised that in the event that a dual/multiple relationship cannot be avoided, mental health counselors take appropriate professional precautions such as informed consent, consultation, supervision and documentation to ensure that their judgment is not impaired and no exploitation has occurred or will occur.

Finally, addiction counselors should not accept as clients, individuals with whom they are involved in an administrative, supervisor or other relationship where they hold the 'power of their position' in the context of the relationship.

Boundary Issues

It is the responsibility of the addiction counselor to maintain appropriate boundaries in the professional relationship with clients.

Professionals should avoid any conduct that could impair their objectivity and professional judgment. They should avoid any conduct that carries the risk and/or appearance of exploitation or potential harm to the client.

Addiction counseling is a professional activity that requires interactions with clients. As a result counselors are advised against hugging and other physical contact that could imply that the counselor has a personal, rather than a professional, relationship with the patient. The avoidance of physical contact, even when it appears appropriate, minimizes the risk of misunderstanding or of allegations of inappropriate contact.

Many of the concerns about personal and professional boundaries have already been addressed above under Harassment and Dual Relationships. Here are a few other areas where counselors should exercise caution:

- Treating patients to whom you are related by blood or legal ties;

- Bartering with patients for the provision of services;

- Supervising applicants for licensure or other training when you are related by blood or legal ties, or when you are having or have previously had a sexual relationship with the trainee;

- Counselors must learn to detect and deflect seductive behaviors of clients. Any concerns should be addressed immediately by pointing to the professional nature of the relationship, and the rules and policies of the organization regarding client behaviors. Counselors should document any such behavior and inform and seek advice from their supervisors.

- Establishing online contact with clients through social networks such as Facebook, Twitter, Hi-5, MySpace, Google Plus+, and Linkedin;

- Counselors should avoid any behaviors that may result in client's mistaking believing that the relationship is one of 'friends'. Thus be careful of all types of social activities with clients. Consider carefully before attending weddings, celebrations (including recovery anniversaries) even for former clients;

- As indicated above, one national study showed that 87% of the counselors and psychotherapists in the study indicated that they had been attracted at least once to their client. Thus, it can be deduced that sexual attraction to clients is a potentially major issue. However, it need not be an issue that devolves into sexual intimacy with clients.

Counselors who experience such feelings for their clients should:

  o Address the issue with their supervisor;

  o Carefully reflect on all comments, behaviors and interactions with the client with a view to avoid future infringements or to correct past mistakes;

  o Carefully plan all sessions with the client;

  o Document and note in extraordinary detail everything that occurs in sessions;

o Go the extra mile in avoiding blurred lines of verbal language, body language, physical distance, dress, etc;

o To the degree possible – whenever possible – keep the door open!

o If the issue becomes a serious distraction – discuss again with the supervisor with the goal of considering a referral. Extreme caution should be exercised at this juncture since the client may be unaware of the reason for the referral and may ultimately feel aggrieved at any such decision – particularly if they perceive that they are benefitting from the counseling relationship.

- Accepting gifts from clients can be dangerous on several levels. Some clients may attempt to use gifts as opportunities to undermine the objectivity and impartiality of counselors. There is a risk of changing the nature of the counseling relationship whereby clients may expect reciprocal favors or gifts.

- Referring patients to services in which you have a financial relationship, without disclosing that you may stand to benefit financially from their use of the service.

- Entering into financial relationships with patients other than their paying for your professional services.

- Inappropriately identifying with clients is sometimes a problem for some addiction counselors. These counselors err when they attempt to establish rapport with clients by identifying with aspects of the client's history, behaviors and/or thoughts. In making these attempts counselors may reveal commonalities that they supposedly share with clients. This is often not only a clinical mistake but an ethical one. Counselors cannot always be certain that the client may receive the communication as expected. Inexperienced counselors may also unwittingly fall into manipulative and conniving web of savvy and experienced clients.

Self-Disclosure

- Self-disclosure refers to a counselor who reveals to a client that they too are in recovery, along with anything else relating to their personal experience from their history. There is a high percentage of people who are in recovery in the field of addiction counseling. It is estimated that as much as 55% of 36,000+ members of the largest national association alcohol and drug counselors are recovering alcoholics and 21% are recovering from some other chemical dependency.

One facet of this mixing of counselors with clients occurs at the local AA or other recovery meeting where both clients and counselors often come not only face to face but take part in the same meeting – sharing their stories and perspectives.

Many recovering professionals see nothing wrong with this scenario and some of them see self-disclosure – within a recovery meeting or in a one-on-one session – as a real benefit to their work. The question that many others ask is: "Who benefits? The client or the counselor." In most cases, self-disclosure, particularly when it takes place in a recovery meeting is for the benefit of the person doing the disclosing. On the other hand, when it takes place in a group or individual counseling session, ostensibly it is for the benefit of the client/s. Or is it? That may be the external and conscious objective of the counselor. But clinical questions remain as to the unconscious objective. Significant clinical questions continue to be asked about the benefits of such disclosure to clients.

In that regard, counselors run the risks of:

o   Clients not understanding the point of the disclosure;

o   Counselors inability to get the right message accepted by the client;

o   The message given or intended might not be the message received;

o   Problems might arise when both are at recovery meetings and issues are revealed that the counselor knows nothing about;

o   Clients may ask themselves or be genuinely confused as to when and whether this person is my colleague or my counselor? Role confusion and role reversals are serious threats to the dynamics of the counseling alliance. Role reversals might occur for example, when a client begins to give the counselor advice on something that the counselor revealed about him/herself. Once roles are reversed, momentary or lasting shifts may occur in the relationship and it might be difficult for the counselor to resume his/her therapeutic role in the relationship.

○ It might potentially be disastrous if the client thinks or believes he/she sees evidence of the counselor slipping.

Before counselors chose to self-disclose, they should consider the following questions:

○ What will this accomplish?

○ How else and in what other ways can I make the therapeutic point?

○ Is the timing right?

○ Am I trying to meet some of my own needs?

○ How can the client personalize and use what I share?

○ How might the client misinterpret my intentions and/or my statements?

Professional Distance

Professional distance refers to the space that addiction counselors maintain between themselves and their clients so that they can perform their duties ethically and professionally. This 'space' that counselors maintain between themselves and their clients helps them to avoid making errors in judgment that may lead to the merging of professional and personal relationships.

Professional distance is also about the constraints that addiction counselors have regarding their level of responsibility for and attachment to client, decisions, choices and outcomes. Professional distance means knowing when to "let go" of client issues.

Here are questions to consider:

- Whose needs are being served, mine or the clients?

- Will this have an impact on the service I am delivering?

- What is my level of comfort in consulting with my supervisor about on any issue with this client?

- How would this be viewed by the client's family, my supervisor, or the court?

- Am I treating this client differently (appointment length, number of times I see the client, issues that I address vs. those that I let slide, personal disclosures)?

- Am I comfortable in documenting *everything* that occurs in the sessions?

- Does the client think that I treat him/her differently?

Professional Power

- Addiction counselors have expert knowledge which not only includes knowledge of addiction treatment principles and practices but also knowledge of resources and systems that the client needs.

- Within the context of the treatment relationship it is generally understood that the counselor is identified with a unique position of power which is embraced and accepted by the client. This position must be carefully managed by the counselor to ensure that the welfare of the client is always the pre-eminent considerations when decisions are made.

- Some counselors develop a sense of personal power within the context of their relationships with clients which can ultimately lead them to make unwise and unethical decisions.

- Professionals are expected to have a high level of responsibility for their interactions with clients and the management of their cases. However, they may also lack control over significant aspects of the system in which they operate including administrative and clinical decisions.

  This paradox of being responsible, while lacking key control can leave some counselors with a lack of confidence in themselves and the system in which they operate. The danger here is that this lack of confidence may be reflected in their interactions with clients and ultimately contribute to the ineffectiveness of counselors.

Client's Vulnerability

- Clients have needs they in many cases they perceive that they cannot take care of themselves. They need help from counselors who then may have power and influence (over the client) which must be used to benefit the client. It is critical that counselors, rather than, embracing this designation of power over the client, inspire the client to understand and get in touch with their own power over their choices/decisions in all aspects of their lives.

- Because clients are searching for resolution of important issues in their lives they are often very open to the influence of others who may project that they have the answers, or whom the clients themselves may believe hold answers or resolutions to their quests.

- In many respects, clients vulnerabilities may extend to their lack of belief in their own self-determination. This also makes them vulnerable to external influences.

Boundary Vulnerabilities of Counselors

Here are questions that counselors should ask themselves:

- Do you have a family member who is chemically dependent or mentally ill? If yes, to what degree does this influence your practice methodology and treatment philosophy?

- Are you recovering from and addiction or mental illness? If yes, how does this influence your interactions with clients. If no, how does this influence your interactions? If no, do you feel less qualified to be an addiction counselor?

- Have you done your own healing work for your own issues?

- What type of client/patient would you dislike or be challenged working with? Why?

- What type of client/patient would prefer to work with? Why?

- What personal life situations/issues may cause a "window of vulnerability" for your usually clear ethical and professional modes of practice?

Decision Making Processes

- Review your professional code of ethics and legal mandates regularly.

- Seek input from a colleague who is widely respected for their knowledge and highly levels of professional and ethical modes of practice.

- Determine the values (motives) involved in your thinking. For example is your decision based on the ethical guidelines or your religious or cultural values?

- Evaluate the long term effects of your choices/ decisions on your clients   .

Organization Responses to Deal with & Prevent Boundary Issues

1. Advocate that the organization develop policies to help avoid serious boundary violations.

2. Encourage the organization's leadership to mandate that staff members periodically audit and review organizational rules and ethics guidelines.

3. Organizations should ensure that all staff benefit from effective clinical supervision.

4. As a matter of policy, organizations should engage in regular professional staff development series to facilitate the ongoing growth in knowledge and skills of staff.

5. Organizations should have internal mechanisms to assist professionals with their own self-care.

6. As a matter of policy and best practices, organizations should respond quickly to any early warning signs of ethical violations.

Ethical Dilemmas

Challenges to your ethical responsibilities and reporting ethical infractions

- Boundaries

- Disclosures

- Therapeutic joining with the client

- Information that can be disclosed

- What to do with professionals who have acted unethically?

- Even though most professions have ethical codes requiring unethical behavior to be reported, professionals do not always report them; Why?

Reluctant Professionals

1. Deny that a colleague may have done something wrong

2. Worried about possible reprisals, especially if it is someone in a position of power

3. Uncomfortable with what they consider 'hearsay' information, reluctant to take action without proof

4. Concerned that their colleague will lose their credentials of even get fired

5. Lack of knowledge about where and how to report unethical conduct

Professional Responsibilities

1. All professionals are responsible for knowing and abiding by the code of ethics.

2. Codes only requires an awareness of the activities

3. It is not your responsibility to determine innocence or guilt. All you have to do is make a report to the appropriate authority.

Principle 10: Inter-Professional Relationships

Addiction counselors are to maintain the highest levels of professional relationships with their colleagues. Counselors must respect the confidential information that is shared with them by other professionals primarily in the best interest of clients, but secondly in the interest of their support of their colleagues. Counselors should not purposefully withhold from other professionals any information or data that has been appropriately released by the client when such information could enhance treatment outcomes.

Addiction counselors must make the best professional effort to support supervisory or consultative team decisions that have been developed to enhance treatment effectiveness.

Counselors must cooperate with 'duly constituted professional ethics committees of their various certification and licensing boards unless they are truly constrained by issues of confidentiality.

Counselors must not in any way exploit their relationships with supervisees, employees, students, research participants or volunteers.

Supervisors

All of the guidelines articulated in this guide apply not only to the interactions of supervisors with clients, but also **apply to and describe exactly** how supervisors should interact with their supervisees.

In general, supervisors must also attend to their administrative, organizational, management and supervisory skills. However, supervisors are specifically responsible for evaluating the performance of supervisees and for promoting and encouraging their professional growth and development as addiction counselors. They have an obligation not only to enhance their own clinical skills but to grow and develop as leaders. Thus, supervisors, in their role as leaders, should schedule regular ongoing performance evaluation meetings.

Principle 11: Remuneration

Addiction counselors should establish financial practices as required by Federal, State and local laws and that exemplify the highest standards expected of certified and licensed professionals.

Financial practices must be developed such that they safeguard the best interests of the client first. Thus, counselors should consider the ability of clients to meet the financial costs of the professional counseling services that are offered.

Counselors should not use the relationships with clients for personal gain or profit beyond what is normally expected of a fee for counseling services, nor should they enter into commercial relationships with clients or other commercial relationships that involve clients at any level.

Counselors should not accept private fees for professional services from clients when such services are being offered through an institution or agency unless clients after being informed of such services, elects to request private services. In any regard, counselors should exercise extraordinary caution in taking private fees from clients who are already receiving services from an institution, or from clients who are eligible to receive 'free' (paid by a third party) services but may not be aware of their eligibility.

Counselors are similarly warned against entering into private counseling arrangements with clients who are either currently enrolled in an agency with which the counselor currently works or has worked in the past.

Principle 12: Societal Obligations

Addiction counselors have a societal obligation to serve as an advocate for individuals who are diagnosed with any substance related disorder.

Addiction counselors should advocate on behalf of their clients with legislators, educators, researchers, health agencies and institutions, treatment agencies, courts and law enforcement, schools and other educational institutions, federal, state and local governments and the general public.

Principles of
Professional Development

Professional Principal 1: Impartiality

Guidelines

- All clients and customers of your agency are entitled to fair and equitable treatment, regardless of their behavior, social status, race, ethnicity, gender, education, or sexual orientation.

- All employees (including clerical and administrative employees) must offer the same level of competent help to all customers and clients.

- While every employee has the right to freedom of association or political expression, he or she does not have the right to impose opinions on clients, customers or colleagues.

- Employees must not only be impartial, but must be seen to be acting impartially by clients and customers.

Professional Principal 2:   Personal Integrity

Guidelines

- The fundamental attitudes and work habits of individual employees are of vital importance.

- Your professional integrity and the integrity of your organization must be ensured at all times.

- Honesty and truthfulness are paramount. Other important character traits on which high levels of integrity are built include: reliability, responsibility, fairness, credibility, openness, decency and honorableness.

- Each individual employee should contribute to the integrity of the entire organization.

Professional Principal 3: Professionalism

Guidelines

- Employment with your organization is a matter of trust. Thus, the general public and your employer has the right to expect you to be trustworthy at all times.

- A professional knows every aspect of his or her job and can provide complete, understandable answers to the questions from clients, other customers and the general public.

- A professional presents a businesslike image of methodical and systematic efficiency. The issue of image is a key one within the field of addiction counselors. Many counselors incorrectly believe that in order to connect with the client they must present an image that is not too distanced from that of the client. Whether in dress or behavior, since counselors are the professionals in the relationship, they must lead the way whether in dress or behavior.

- A professional never criticizes a co-worker in public, or in private with a client or other customer. Additionally, the professional never ever denigrates a customer in any forum.

- A professional artfully uses high level skills to resolve conflicts through informal negotiation and mediation techniques. This indicates that conflict resolution and mediation are critical skills that addiction counseling

71

professionals should discuss.

- A professional is expected to have high levels of knowledge and skills related to his/her area of responsibility. Therefore, he/she assumes responsibility for his/her continuous growth and development. This is another crucial factor in the addiction counseling field where some counselors have been criticized because they have not stayed abreast of the developments in scientifically based treatment approaches.

- A professional must not only willingly embrace change, but must become a skilled agent of change. Essentially, treatment for any substance dependence or abuse is about change. Thus, counselors ought to be experts at coaching or counseling clients on how they can change from users or abusers to being drug free.

Professional Principle 4: Confidentiality

Guidelines

- Sensitive information acquired by *all agency employees* in the course of discharging their official duties should never be revealed until it is made a matter of public record. In the addiction counseling field this is an integral part of the Health Insurance Portability and Accountability Act (HIPAA) which applies to all staff within an agency which handles private health information of customers/clients.

- Sometimes breaches of confidentiality do not involve intentional disclosure of official records but are the result of innocent and casual remarks. However, such remarks can seriously compromise the privacy of clients' health information, or confidential organizational data.

- Employees must exert great care when establishing dual relationships with colleagues and/or customers. In the counseling professions, under most circumstances dual relationships between counselors and clients are clearly prohibited. Less clear are the relationships that other employees within the same agency can have with clients and customers. This situation needs to be clarified in agency policies.

- Employees in the helping professions must break confidentiality to report human rights violations including violence and abuse against minors, residents of institutions,

73

the elderly, and people with disabling conditions. Another exception to confidentiality occurs when threats are made against self or others. This obligation applies to all staff within health related agencies.

Professional Principle 5: Impropriety

Guidelines

- Employees must avoid any mode of conduct that casts doubt on the integrity and impartiality of the organization and those who are employed therein.

- Employees must conduct themselves in a manner that inspires the public confidence in the role they play in pursuit of their organization's goals.

- Proper conduct involves daily and scrupulous affirmation of ethical principles and observance of all laws, and organizational rules, policies and procedures.

Professional Principle 6: Appearance of Impropriety

Guidelines

- Employees are expected to refrain from engaging not only in improper behavior, but also in behavior that others might perceive to be improper.

- Any activity that gives the impression that employees can be improperly influenced in the performance of their official duties is prohibited.

- Employees are required to live up to a higher standard of ethical behavior than the general public.

Professional Principle 7: Duty to Serve

Guidelines

- A major goal of all employees is to provide full, accurate and timely information to all customers and specifically to clients.

- When giving information to customers, whether orally or in writing, employees should present it in an easy to understand format and avoid profession-specific jargon whenever possible.

- Staff members are employed to serve and should strive to do everything possible to make things easier for clients and customers rather than for themselves or the organization.

- Both external and internal customers should have their information service needs met with the same levels of dispatch and consideration. In other words, counselors should treat their administrative colleagues with the same levels of professional service that they provide clients.

- Employees in the helping professions hold their clients' best interest as their primary obligation. They should also as important the principle of "doing no harm".

Professional Principle 8: Competency

Guidelines

- Staff members are encouraged to participate in professional activities and associations, and especially to take advantage of internal and external educational programs to improve their personal and professional skills.

- Organizations and their employees must perform at the highest levels despite the constant urgent operations and changes which occur within the organization, community and/or the marketplace. Because clients' lives can be at stake within the addiction counseling field, counselors have a very high obligation to be always at their professional best.

- Managers at all levels should initiate, organize and supervise ongoing professional growth programs which must include the study of the organization's code of ethics, laws and regulations covering the field, and profession specific ethical guidelines and professional modes and standards of practice.

Professional Principle 9: Diversity & Cultural Competence

Guidelines

- *Equal access* to the organization's services and products and, *fair and equal treatment* for all are the **cornerstones** of most laws and the best business principles and practices.

- Employees are expected to treat each other and each user of the organization's services equally and with *compassion* and *empathy*.

- Employees may not discriminate against each other or a user of organization's services on the basis of age, disability, race, religion, national origin, language, sexual orientation, legal status, personal appearance or any other identifying characteristic.

- Employees must *demonstrate* compassion and empathy when dealing with accused felons, child abusers, spouse abusers, participants in painful dissolutions, those grieving from an injury or loss of a loved one, or people experiencing any of the numerous kinds of human pain, disability, dysfunction or social condition.

- Employees must discourage and *expose* discrimination wherever it exists.

Cultural Competence Recommendations

Addiction counselors should:

- Form and test hypotheses about a culturally different patient's issues, rather than making premature conclusions about that client and his or her culture. Be aware of and understand and acknowledge your own limits of knowledge of the client's cultural history and therefore the limitations of your hypotheses.

- Generalize and individualize. Know when to generalize about certain client behaviors and when to individualize. This is a decidedly delicate skill that can only come as a result of developing cultural expertise over time.

- Develop culturally specific expertise – a thorough understanding of the specific cultural group's most prevalent in your geographical area or community from which you are likely to be getting clients.

- Ask clients for help in understanding the value systems which they embrace. And, make sure clients feel that any cultural differences they may have with you are respected and acknowledged (by the counselor) during the counseling process.

- Remember your commitment to the individual. Counselors who focus too much on an cultural feature, such as skin color, may form a one-dimensional image of a client and ignore the unique and multilayered character that a person brings to the counseling relationship.

- Engage in on-going self-assessment. What are your personal positions, biases, beliefs, and perspectives which may help or hinder your effectiveness.

- Identify and acknowledge how you express your individual heritage, identity, values, beliefs, faith and biases.

- Study concepts relevant to diversity, such as power, privilege, and prejudice.

- Form cross-cultural relationships based on trust, caring, and mutual benefits. Become involved with diverse individuals outside of work and classroom environments.

- Acquire knowledge about and be willing to listen to other perspectives – be they political, religious, social, ethnic, psychological or – just different.

- Recognize different and similar learning, communication, motivational, and decision-making strategies and styles.

- Develop effective responses to challenges posed by new (to you) attitudes, emotive responses, behaviors, or thinking.

- Take responsibility for your own personal, professional, and educational development on these issues.

- Develop the ability and willingness to challenge prejudice, discrimination and oppression wherever you may find them particularly when doing so as a professional and on behalf of clients that you serve.

- Make a life-long commitment to respecting the rights and dignity of cultural groups that different from your own.

- Develop effective skills for cross-cultural verbal and non-verbal communication. Pay particular attention to those non-verbal that you accept as 'the norm' (such as: shaking hands, hugging, looking in someone' eyes, etc.) Other issues to pay attention to may be group related 'norms' such as praying before the start of a session or meeting, and joining hands in certain group activities.

- Risk changing 'me' as a result of exposure to 'them'.

- Study and reflect on membership and identification with diverse cultural group worldviews and history. Understand that specific groups may have varied beliefs and practices within their own group. Develop knowledge base about various cultures, lifestyles, and multiple perspectives within cultures, cultural identity development and the global community.

- Focus all efforts on the ultimate goal of developing and enhancing your skills (cultural competence and cross-cultural effectiveness) for the distinct benefit of your culturally different clients.

Professional Principle 10: Harassment

Guidelines

- Employees at all levels are to refrain from making sexual advances and *insinuations* to anyone – clients, other customers or colleagues. They must avoid behaviors that are inappropriate and offensive, *or those that could be perceived* as such.

- It is the ethical responsibility of organizations to have a clear and unambiguous written and published policy against harassment and discrimination.

Professional Principle 11: Technology

Guidelines

- Employees are to treat information received and/or retained in electronic files like any other official document.

- Great care should be taken in the electronic transmission of confidential information such that the *intended reader/receiver* **is** the *actual recipient.*

- Care should also be taken that electronic data preserves both the integrity of the company/organization and the employee. Such data would not embarrass the company/organization, the sender (or any other person) *if it is read by an unintended recipient.*

- Employees may **not** install personal software or equipment without prior approval of the company's executive officer, nor shall they take copyrighted software outside the company's premises for *personal use.*

- Questions about the ownership of intellectual property should be directed to an administrator/executive officer.

Record Keeping & Documentation

Key Guidelines

1. Responsibility for records: Although agencies and employers assume this responsibility, individual counselors may be held liable for the maintenance and retention of client records.

2. Counselors are responsible for the content of the records, therefore the counselor must ensure that the information that he/she places there is correct.

3. Confidentiality of records: The counselor must take reasonable steps to ensure and maintain the privacy of information resulting from services provided.

4. As indicated in the section under "Informed Consent", counselors must inform clients of the nature and extent of the maintenance and retention of records.

5. Maintenance of records: The counselor must organize and maintain records while ensuring their accuracy. Counselors are also responsible for ensuring that others who have legitimate access to the records use them appropriately.

6. Security: The counselor takes appropriate steps to protect records from unauthorized access, damage and destruction.

7. Retention of records: The counselor strives to be aware of

the applicable laws and regulations and to retain records for the period required by legal, regulatory, institutional and ethical requirements.

8. Electronic records: Electronic records should be created and maintained in a way that is designed to protect their security, integrity, confidentiality and appropriate access as well as their compliance with applicable legal and ethical requirements.

9. Preserving the context of records: The counselor strives to be attentive to the situational context in which records are created and how that context may influence the content and disposition of those records as well as how the records could be used in the best interest of the client.

10. Record keeping in organizational settings: Counselors working in organizational settings strive to follow the record keeping policies and procedures of the organization as well as all legal and ethical guidelines.

Record Keeping Guidelines

The client record should include as appropriate and relevant:

1. Client name

2. Client address

3. Home and office telephone numbers

4. Date of the counselor's first contact with the client and the nature of the contact

5. Demographic data, gender age, etc.

6. An accurate record of the evaluation and treatment of the client and any significant changes of treatment over the course of service

7. Documents such as contracts and consent forms

8. The date and nature of each billed service contact

9. Names of individuals with whom the psychologist formally consulted about the client, including reasons for consultation, dates and relevant consent forms

10. A copy of all test or other evaluation reports prepared as a part of the professional relationship

11. Narrative of all significant outside billable contacts between counselor and others

12. Billing and payment history, including insurance payment

The ongoing record should also include, as appropriate and relevant:

1. Referral source, if any;

2. Family data (marital status, custodial and other information, if pertinent);

3. Special information or conditions that might have an impact on treatment or cause the client stress (e.g. sensory impairment, socioeconomic status, physical impairment or other special circumstances);

4. Observations about the client's language ability if relevant (e.g. the client does not speak English, cannot read, etc.);

5. Medical/psychiatric history (pertinent illnesses and treatment);

6. History of substance use, including use of prescription medications (with dosages), and current medications being taken;

7. Use of alcohol and nature of use; patterns of abuse and history of treatment received;

8. Name of client's personal physician, psychologist, and other counselors. Names of programs which the client has attended;

9. Telephone number of someone to contact in emergency situations;

10. Documentation of any mandated disclosures of confidential information with the required fully completed consent form signed by the client;

11. Presenting complaint, diagnosis or reasons for request of services;

12. Plan for services, updated as appropriate (e.g. treatment plan, supervision plan, intervention schedule);

13. The record may also include:
    a. Client responses or reactions to professional interventions;
    b. Current risk factors in relation to dangerousness to self or others;
    c. All treatment modalities employed;

    d. Emergency interventions (e.g. specially scheduled sessions, hospitalizations);

    e. Plans for future/recommended interventions;

    f. Information describing the qualitative aspects of the professional – client interactions which may be clinically or legally significant;

g. Assessment or summary of data (e.g. psychological testing, structured interviews, behavioral ratings, client behavior logs);

h. Case related telephone, mail, fax, and e-mail contacts;

i. Relevant cultural and socio-political factors.

Important Issues Related To Documentation

- "If it was not written, it was not done."

- Think before you write.

- Use limited abbreviations.

- The record is a legal document.

- Date and time on all notes very important.

- Time is the time of contact.

- Do not use white out in charts.

- When correcting errors, mark one line over word(s), write the word "error" and your initials.

12 General Mistakes Counselors Must Avoid

1. Lying or in any way misrepresenting the facts about any of your performances, activities, behaviors or relationships that potentially could impact the client, company/organization.

2. Blaming others for personal mistakes or those of the people you supervise.

3. Divulging personal or confidential information to peers, senior managers, employees, customers, competitors, or the general public without the appropriately executed consent.

4. Permitting, or failing to report, violations of any laws or regulations.

5. As a supervisor, protecting sub-standard performers from corrective discipline or termination.

6. Condoning or failing to report the theft or misuse of company property or of any infringements or violations of the ethical guidelines covering Addiction Counselors.

7. Suppressing grievances or complaints whether they are initiated by clients, colleagues or by members of the general public.

8. Covering up on-the-job accidents and failing to report health and safety hazards.

9. Ignoring or violating the company's commitments to clients,

employees and customers.

10. Passing on information or ideas from clients, customers or colleagues as your own.

11. Becoming involved in potentially harmful dual relationships with clients (or their family members), supervisees, or customers.

12. Harassing, pressuring or attempting to unduly influence people you supervise, clients or customers to be involved in personal, social or commercial relationships.

Ten Rules for Counseling Professionals

1. Consider the needs of others, not just your own. Remember that you have to give to get, and that life is better when you live it as a win/win process.

2. Never forget just who you and your organization are. You are part of the community and a thread in the fabric of society. Don't do those things that common sense will tell you will cause the fabric to unravel.

3. Obey rules, laws, and cultural standards, or advocate that they be changed. Remember, however, that you can be unethical without breaking the law. Use common sense and assess the potential damage of an unethical act or the violation of moral standards in advance. Violations are not worth it in the long run.

4. Test your thinking frequently. Ask yourself, "Is this the right thing to do? Is it fair? Is it honest? Is there a better way? Am I taking the high road?"

5. Don't lose your objectivity. This is a simple statement, but a tough order. What is right, what is fair, what is in your best interest may be a lot of different things. Be sure you put your biases aside and look at all aspects of the issue. And as a counseling professional, remember that the best interest of the client is primary.

6. Include good ethical practices in all your plans. Don't leave them to chance. Think through who you are and how you

want to be seen and known. Bringing these considerations to the surface and keeping them there will enable you to maintain good ethical practice.

7. Recognize the ethical implications of issues *as they arise*.

8. Correct unethical practices that may have previously been unrecognized or ignored.

9. When making decisions, keep the ethical principles at the forefront.

10. Communicate the need for applying ethical principles at all levels of your organization.

References & Bibliography

Ahia, C. E., & Martin, D. (1993). *The Danger-to-Self-or Others Exception to Confidentiality.* Alexandria, VA: American Counseling Association.

American Counseling Association. (1995). *Code of Ethics and Standards of Practice.* Alexandria, VA.

American Psychological Association. (1995). *Ethical Standards of Psychologists and Code of Conduct.* Washington, DC

Anderson, B. S. (1996) *The Counselor and the Law* (4th ed.). Alexandria, VA: American Counseling Association.

Arthur, G. L., & Swanson, C. D. (1993). *Confidentiality and Privileged Communication.* Alexandria, VA: American Counseling Association.

Atkinson, D. R., Morten, G., & Sue, D. W. (Eds.). (1993). *Counseling American Minorities: A Cross-Cultural Perspective* (4th ed.). Dubuque, IA: Brown and Benchmark.

American Society of Addiction Medicine. (2000). Public policy statement on confidentiality in physician illness. *Journal of Addictive Diseases* 19(2): 123-125.

Association for Advanced Training in the Behavioral Sciences. (1994). *Ethics Manual.* California.

Barton A; Quinn C. (2002). Risk management of groups or respect for the individual? Issues for information sharing and confidentiality in Drug Treatment and Testing Orders. *Drugs: Education, Prevention and Policy* 9(1): 35-43.

Bjarnason T; Adalbjarnardottir S. (2000). Anonymity and confidentiality in school surveys on alcohol, tobacco, and cannabis use. *Journal of Drug Issues* 30(2): 335-343.

Brock, G. W. (Ed.). (1994). *American Association for Marriage and Family Therapy ethics casebook.* Washington, DC: American Association for Marriage and Family Therapy.

Brody JL; Waldron HB. (2000). Ethical issues in research on the treatment of adolescent substance abuse disorders. *Addictive Behaviors* 25(2): 217 -228.

Corey, G., Corey, M. & Callanan, P. (2010). *Issues and Ethics in the Helping Professions* Belmont, CA: Brooks Cole.

Corey, G. (2008) *Theory and Practice of Counseling & Psychotherapy.* Belmont, CA: Thomson Higher Education.

Recovering and Non-recovering Substance Abuse Counselors. Journal of Counseling and Development, vol. 77, (3), p. 330 - 338.

Grobma, L. (1999). *A Day in the Life of Social Workers 2ⁿᵈ Edition).* New York: White Hat Communications.

Hatherleigh Guide To Ethics in Therapy. (1997). New York: Hatherleigh Press.

Herlihy, B. & Remley, D. P. (2009). *Ethical, Legal and Professional Issues in Counseling.* New York: Pearson Education.

Herlihy, B. & G. Corey (Eds.) (2006). *ACA Ethical Standards Casebook* (5th ed.). Alexandria, VA: American Counseling Association.

Herlihy, B. & G. Corey (Eds.) (2006). *Boundary Issues in Counseling: Multiple Roles and Responsibilities.* Alexandria, VA: American Counseling Association.

Keith-Spiegel, P. & Koocher, G. P. (1985). *Ethics in Psychology: Professional Standards and Cases.* New York: Random House.

Maynard, A. & Beckett, C. (2005). *Values & Ethics in Social Work.* San Francisco: Sage Publications.

National Association of Alcoholism and Drug Abuse Counselors. *Ethical Standards of Alcoholism and Drug Abuse Counselors.* Arlington, VA.

National Association of Social Workers. (1996). *Code of Ethics.* Washington, DC.

Pope, K. & Vasquez, M. (2010) *Ethics in Psychotherapy and Counseling: A Practical Guide.* San Francisco, CA: Wiley & Sons.

Reamer, F. (2006) *Social Work Values & Ethics.* New York: Columbia University Press.

Reamer, F. (2006) *Ethical Standards in Social Work: A Review of the NASW Code of Ethics.* Washington, DC: NASW Press.

Rubin, S. (1997). Balancing Duty to Client and Therapist in Supervision: Clinical, Ethical, and Training Issues. The Clinical Supervisor, vol. 16, (1), p. 1-24

Scott CG. (2000). Ethical issues in addiction counseling. *Rehabilitation Counseling Bulletin* 43(4): 209-214.

Sue, D. W., Ivey, A. E., & Pedersen, P. B. (1996). *A Theory of Multicultural Counseling and Therapy.* Pacific Grove, CA: Brooks/Cole.

Taleff, M.J. (2009) *Advanced Ethics for Addiction Professionals.* New York, NY: Springer Publishing Company, LLC.

Tyler, J. M. & Tyler, C. L. (1997). Ethics in supervision: Managing supervisee rights and supervisor responsibilities. In *The Hatherleigh Guide to Ethics in Therapy* (pp. 76-94). New York: Hatherleigh Press.

Weddle M; Kokotailo P. (2002) Adolescent substance abuse: Confidentiality and consent. *Pediatric Clinics of North America* 49(2): 301-316.

Wrenn, C. G. (1985). The culturally encapsulated counselor revisited. In P. Pedersen (Ed.), *Handbook of Cross-Cultural Counseling and Therapy* (pp. 323-328). Wesport, CT: Greenwood Press.

.

Life Management Publishing
Copyright © 2012

www.Prevent-Drug-Abuse.com

www.SpeakTrain.com

www.SpeakAndTrain.com

www.HealYourHurt.com

www.HelpForDomesticViolence.com